Cats' Only Vice Is Destruction

Written by Dr Sam

Illustrated by David Anderson

PREFACE

I would like to dedicate this book to Major
who died to no fault of his own,
you will always be in my heart.

Some of the proceeds of this book
will be donated to animal shelters.

Where is this silly human going?
Hope they feed us before they go roaming.
Hold on, they cannot leave the home.
Oh no they cannot even leave the dome.

Oh my gosh they are here with us.
They better not cry and make a fuss.
Don't use my kitty litter today!
I'm already upset you are here to stay.

Not really, I have to think of a plan
To run around as fast as we can,
Scratch their sofa and chairs…whipeeeee!
They are not amused, but we want to be free.

I am not going to be nice and kind.
I'll scratch and piss on everything I find.
The human is not leaving the house anymore.
I have to pretend and purr for amore.

The human just sits there and eats.
I cannot go out to the garden and cheat
Or play with the neighbour who is nice and old,
So I will have to stay and do as I'm told.

If I see my kitty litter is used
Someone's bed is going to be wet and abused.
I will pee on all that I find
And believe me, I am not going to be kind!

Why is this human sitting in my chair?
All I can do is crouch on the ground and stare.
Hopefully they will get up and move
But I I have to be quick and smooth.

I don't understand why they sit and stare at
a box,
Don't they know they're supposed to move
like a fox
Fast and quick to keep the muscles healthy
and strong?
So get up and move, it doesn't take too long.

I need to throw a hairball their way,
So I can be alone without being a stray.
They have to clean up the mess that I'll make
So please get off your butt for goodness sake.

Why are these humans not out free?
I just want to lay quietly in my tree.
Phone ringing, door slamming, lady sings.
Why can't they fly out the window with
their wings?

I have to see how we can get their attention,
No worry about getting caught since I can't
get detention.
Smashing a glass from the countertop
Is a good way to start until they stay stop!

Glass all over the kitchen floor for them
to walk,
I can't see their mouths, do they even talk?
I'll keep running around all over the living
room floor,
Not sitting like them lazy as a boring flat door.

Masks, masks, all over the living room space,
Making a mess and not even changing
their pace.
How long can we live like this, it's driving
me insane,
Someone please help me because these
humans are a pain!

Ignoring the chores, looking at the
magical box,
I'm trying to play around them and be sneaky
as a fox.
Glass is still on the floor for all to adore,
They just keep eating and now they are
making a s'more!

We had so much peace and could sleep on
their desks,
But now we have to sit and help them find
their specs.
Talking to their computer boxes again,
and loud!
I want to sleep quietly floating on a cloud.

I will hide so they think I am lost,
I want peace no matter the cost.
Walking around with no humans around
Is the best in the world for me, I found.

I will not meow so I will not be found.
Making sure no one else is around
Since I do not want them to find
My best place to hide, if you do not mind.

Who are these new humans with masks,
We can't see them but they're doing
some tasks.
Sleeping, eating, and drinking all day,
We want to be alone, eat and just play.

The humans do not like to sleep.
I just want to eat my kibbles and creep
Around the house late at night
But these humans just want to have a fight.

We have to find a way to win!
Let's find a plan and a way to begin
To find a way back to normal.
But we have to live together so be formal.

Okay, guys, do we have a plan?
I need to look around and scan,
For a human so they do not see
What we are about to do and be free.

Oh no, the masked human is still around,
Let's lay down and pretend to be found.
They will have no idea about our plan
To piss on their books and not in the can!

They will have to leave the house to find
Another book, but maybe a different kind.
We are so happy for when they go out.
We can play and laugh and run and shout!

This pandemic is such a pain.
For us cats it is a stain,
Just like we can make on their beds.
We want them to leave and use their heads.

How long is this going to be?
Sleeping cats is all that you should see,
Not upset meowing; so go out please
So we can get back to our lives with ease!

The humans are lying in their bed again.
It's cold outside and here comes the rain.
I will curl up by their crusty and cold feet.
I wish they would go so we can meet.

Purring and kneading is all I do,
Helping the human and his friend too.
Making them feel calm and special as can be
But they are here and nobody to see!

My plan is beginning to pay off.
The masks are as annoying as a flock.
Shall I smash another glass from
the countertop?
My plan might fail and become a flop.

When is this madness going to end?
The humans with us just do not blend.
Long-term contact is not a good thing.
It was a few years or maybe a fling.

◆ FriesenPress

One Printers Way
Altona, MB R0G 0B0
Canada

www.friesenpress.com

ISBN
978-1-03-915158-1 (Hardcover)
978-1-03-915157-4 (Paperback)
978-1-03-915159-8 (eBook)

1. POETRY, CANADIAN

Distributed to the trade by The Ingram Book Company

CPSIA information can be obtained
at www.ICGtesting.com
Printed in the USA
BVHW090932230123
656819BV00002B/11

9 781039 151581